The Presence of One Word

Andrea Potos

Fernwood
PRESS

The Presence of One Word

©2025 by Andrea Potos

Fernwood Press
Newberg, Oregon
www.fernwoodpress.com

All rights reserved. No part may be reproduced
for any commercial purpose by any method without
permission in writing from the copyright holder.

Printed in the United States of America

Cover and page design: Eric Muhr
Cover art: Junel Mujar on Unsplash
Author photo: Michael Slater

ISBN 978-1-59498-173-9

In *The Presence of One Word*, we find poems powerful in their well-crafted expression of love—for her mother, grandmother, friends, places that moved her in Ireland or Greece or just her own or her grandmother's house. Even empathy and compassion for a tiny spider. She writes many short, pithy poems that catch in the mind and shine there.

—Marge Piercy
author of *On the Way Out, Turn Off the Light*
and *Sleeping with Cats*

In her latest collection, *The Presence of One Word*, Andrea Potos invites us into a world of loving comfort. We willingly travel to these tender places, like the presence of her Yaya's welcoming voice. These poems are infused with ancestral memory, a feast for the senses. Potos takes us to other worlds in her writing, whether it be through family connections, the wonder of nature's majesty, or musings on past poets. For loved ones lost, Potos has a beautiful way of describing liminal spaces, "as if the sunrise / had found its home as she stepped through." We are graced with awe and wonder in this gorgeous collection. With each poem, she is "tapping / from inside the egg / into an astounded world." Potos reminds us to hold close "the deep cup of time in your palms." Through these shared stories of belonging, we all belong.

—Cristina M. R. Norcross
founding editor of *Blue Heron Review*
author of *The Sound of a Collective Pulse*

These are poems of wonder and reverence, tenderness and gratitude. Potos beautifully conjures the lives of family and friends and brings alive beloved literary predecessors, painters, and musicians. As we move through this collection, she beckons us to "kneel down in the deep, fragrant grasses, / make a bed for your body where the summer / is still singing your name." Despite the losses we suffer, this book celebrates the pleasures of being alive in a world that still holds "some stray atoms" of the love and joy and genius of those who have gone before us, those who still light the way. It is a book of great gladness.

—Marilyn Annucci
author of *The Arrows That Choose Us*

In Andrea Potos's gentle collection of poems, she returns to familiar characters: Emily D., the Brontë sisters, her mother, and her yaya. Yet these poems are as new and as fresh as poems written for her recently lost friend, Rosemary. Readers will be taken to Ireland, Vienna, and Brontë's moor. They'll visit Lake Michigan, jacarandas in Los Angeles, and a "green" cemetery. All these poems are written with elegance and grace "as if the egg of Wonder was cracked open / and spilling its secret astonishments."

—**Karla Huston**
Wisconsin Poet Laureate 2017–2018
and author of *Ripple, Scar, and Story*

for Rosemary, in memory and presence

Contents

Acknowledgments 11
Daily Practice 13
Assistance 14
Yaya's Telephone 15
A Belated Thank You to Miss Joanne Martins of Cathedral Square Publishing Company in Milwaukee, Wisconsin, circa 1971 16
Yaya's Dresser 17
On Our Way to My Grandfather's Village 18
Making the Greek Meatballs 19
Against Despair 20
Threshold 21
Quiet in Winter 22
Go Where the Door Is Open, She Said 23
Midwestern Summer 24
Late Apology 25
Poem for Lake Michigan 26
Waiting Beside My Father 27

When My Mother Called 28
Returning to the Old Neighborhood After Thirty Years .. 29
Upon Waking 30
For My Friend Gone On 31
For the Thin Places 32
Eternity 33
The Notebooks of Other Women Poets 34
Visiting the Brontës Again 35
After Twenty Years 35
While in the Yorkshire Dales 36
Writerly Dream 37
The Last Unread Poems of Charlotte Brontë,
    March 2022 38
On the Burren 39
When Asked Why Do I Keep Wanting
    to Return to Ireland 40
After Learning My Friend Has Died 41
To This Day 42
After My Friend's Death, Her Husband Tells Me to Take
    Whatever I Want from Her Bookshelves 43
My Friend's Heart 44
A List 45
How She Might Have Left 46
Christmas List for Santa 47
Daughter, Leaving Again 48
For the Tiny Spider Squashed Inside the Pages of
    Poems by Mary Oliver 49
Praise Song for My Mother 50
The Presence of One Word 51
On Being Asked Again if My Daughter
    Is an Only Child 52
Fiona Penelope in the World 53
Song of the Lark 54
When the Consolation of a Word
    Comes to You 55

At the Green Sanctuary and Natural Path Cemetery 56
Walking the Brontë Moor in Spring..................................57
Girls at the Piano 58
To Do, Morning 59
Coffeehouses in Vienna..60
In Mozart's Apartment...61
Reading the Spanish Poets 62
January Sighting 63
Another Mid-Range Hotel...64
In the Morning Quiet I Hear My Mother Speaking...........65
My Mother and Gratitude 66
Finding My Grandmother on a Greek Island 67
Morning Gladness 68

Title Index 69
First Line Index...73

Acknowledgments

Grateful acknowledgment is made to these journals where some of these poems first appeared, some of them in slightly different form:

Adanna Journal, Bearings Online, CALYX Journal, Delta Poetry Review, Kosmos Quarterly, Literary Mama, Midwest Quarterly, One Art, Quill & Parchment, Paterson Literary Review, Plainsongs, Poetry Breakfast, Poetry East, Poem, Potomac Review, Portage Magazine, Presence, Rosebud, Silver Birch Press, Soul-Lit, Spiritus, and my previous collections, *Yaya's Cloth* (Iris Press), and *Two Emilys* (Kelsay Books).

> *Work of sight is done, now*
> *go and do heart work*
> *on all the images within you.*
>
> —Rainer Maria Rilke, from "Turning-Point"

> *Joy–it's not just a gift. In a sense it's also*
> *a duty, a task to fulfill.*
> *Courage.*
>
> —Anna Kamienska, from *Astonishments*

> *Remember, home*
> *is not where you live but where you are loved.*
>
> —Floyd Skloot, from "The Fall Term"

Daily Practice

Some mornings all I do
is write down words—*cistern,
tribal, cached*—copying them
from sprawled pages of books
across my desk, words that call out—
*glimmerings, cursive, saffron,
heartwood*—holding me in place
as if to say *listen*, you may need me
someday, I might offer you another way
toward beauty, or even beyond.

Assistance

after Joy Harjo

When I pick up my pen
and spread my notebook open,
I rely on the assistance of air,
stillness cradled in quiet.
I depend on coffee,
bitter-tinged and milk-sweet.
I hear writer-ancestors, beginning
with Emily and Louisa who knew me
when I was a fledging girl.

I depend on the rooms of my heart, creaking doors
and windows ajar to the weather. Oh,
and look here, now, comes my grandmother
with her basket full of yarn she will crochet
into another warm and beautiful song;
here comes my mother with a white flower
in the side part of her auburn hair, she is telling me:
I will always love you more than anything.

Yaya's Telephone

Weighty and black, substantial
to raise to the ear; her hands lifting
the heavy receiver to hear my *Hi, Yaya*
from across the city. Three times a day
I'd called to tell her—what?
my pet turtle climbing out
of his plastic island, another batch of snails
unmoving in their tank;
my father's scrumptious malted milkshakes,
my mother's new sequined dress for the party.
She was my landing place. I don't recall ever asking:
How are you, Yaya? She who arrived in America
as a bride of nineteen with no English, who lost her son
when he was on the cusp of four years old
so many years before I arrived.
444-2065 was all I knew, invisible wires
singing still with her voice.

A Belated Thank You to Miss Joanne Martins of Cathedral Square Publishing Company in Milwaukee, Wisconsin, circa 1971

You must have guessed how, at eleven years old, I craved
to be Jo March, scribbling in a garret,
mice scuffling under the floorboards, a heap of apple cores
beside me while rain battered the windowpanes.
By hand I wrote my 103-page novel modeled
not secretly enough after *Little Women*,
and I mailed it off to you.
Bless you Miss Martin for writing me back
three weeks later, for your neatly typed
bullet points of advice: Keep this manuscript
in a safe place, every month reread, you'll be surprised
at the improvements you can make.
Read as much as you can, get a library card.
When you describe an object or person, pretend
you are talking to someone who is blind.
Save your money and invest in a typewriter—a must!
Or ask your parents for one for Christmas.
When you tell your story, write as if
you are talking to a friend, the way you would talk
about something that happened at school.
A writer must always remember
his best friend is the reader. Please do not be
discouraged at receiving your first rejection.

Yaya's Dresser

It seemed to reign
over one half of a whole wall;
its curved drawers were polished
mahogany waves inlaid
with small vines.
Pulling open the top drawer
required all of my childhood weight
to unleash unmistakable scents—
talcum powder and perfumes
of Emeraude, English Lavender.
And then to stroke the neat stacks
of her handkerchiefs, her hand-embroidered linen
with pink thread—great cursive A's—
A for her name *Aristea*, and A, I imagined,
for mine. I couldn't see into my own
long-into-the-future *Alexandra*.
In open satin compartments lay her earrings—
silver clip-ons, faceted rhinestones and lapis beads,
one set a curved pod of tiny oyster pearls.
My fingers would settle and sift through them,
inside that cached belonging
of our feminine world,
staying as long as I could.

On Our Way to My Grandfather's Village

Roumeli, Greece

We stalled in traffic—a line of goats
tinkling their bells as they made
a relaxed gait across the narrow road.
They turned to notice us, no time to hurry.
The land held the clock, and we
were only its visitants.

A few more leaning, mountain curves,
and the village appeared—
warm slate rooftops, mottled gray stones
of the houses where my grandfather was born
more than a century ago, and from his memory—
the reading lamps of the stars.

Making the Greek Meatballs

patting meat into small mounds
for *kefthedes*,
rolling them on a plate
sprinkled with flour,
laying them gently as if to bed
in a warm skillet becoming hot,
waiting for the sizzle, butter goldening
to brown, aromas of my grandmother's
garden parsley, oregano, and onion;
fresh lamb and beef
becoming one, spirits
widening with anticipation
and every holy sense

Against Despair

My grandmother wept at her kitchen sink
for her son, dead at three years old;
through her long life, she crocheted ninety-seven afghans,
sewed my dresses,
my mother's pillows and drapes,
cooked the succulent Greek chicken,
the *spanokopita* and *pastiscio*
for dozens at her Sunday table.

My grandfather in 1943
lost all his savings,
lay prone in his bed for weeks;
his youngest child would peek through the crack
in the door to see him, before
he rose to work sixteen hours
every day in the Harmony Diner

where my twin aunts scampered
behind the counter to build themselves
sundaes with extra cherries,
and my sixteen-year-old mother
sat upstairs in the office
becoming a grown-up,
typing the daily specials:
hot turkey with mashed potatoes and gravy,
grilled pork chops on a toasted bun,
layer cake a la mode, double malted milk,
and coffee, always coffee, five cents a cup
in those days, guaranteed strong
and hot, infinitely refillable.

Threshold

Postpartum

That January day I stood
as if iced in
the grayed winter dawn,

behind me, my grandmother
waving goodbye to our world,
nodding *yes*

toward my newborn, waiting,
wordless, for me
to carry her across.

Quiet in Winter

This winter quiet
is singular among quiets,
as if the air is filled
with hidden landscape,
and a snow queen
from the oldest tale
is stilled inside her carriage.

A forest of iridescence surrounds her.
Solitude is the silence
of her visible breath.

Go Where the Door Is Open, She Said

Turn away from
the hurdled thresholds,

the shut doors and folded shutters,
those places where there isn't any washing

on the lines strung from windows—
no voices of the grandmothers chiming from within,

no tablecloths or towels, no trousers or nightgowns waving
in quiet breezes like invitations to arrive.

Midwestern Summer

The quickest way to the pool
was to cross our street and make a diagonal
across the green of Lions Park. Just past
the school where I'd once escaped from
kindergarten to find my way back to my mom
was the mesmerizing aquamarine,
babysitters and mothers lounging
with their Coppertone, their stacks of *Woman's Day*
and *Seventeen* beside them, near the snack bar that had
the best burger I'd ever had, unwrapped from cellophane
and heated somehow, crunchy on the outside with a squeeze
of ketchup inside it, what I craved after all the hours
of splashing and dunking and hosting underwater
tea parties in the shallow end, a mermaid who couldn't do
a decent crawl or breaststroke yet it didn't matter because
I knew I belonged in the wavery blue shallows, bubbles rising
all around me until I popped like a happy cork to the surface
between air and water, the wavering thin threshold between
    worlds.

Late Apology

50 years later

to the gleaming fat June bug
I scrunched
under my small bare foot
on my way to the Ferris wheel
across the street from my house.
I can still see the smooth black shine
of your armor that failed you
just as I landed.

Oh creature of obsidian summer—
forgive me—I only had eyes for the twinkling
lights that twirled in the dusky nearness
while the moon, ascending,
must have eyed us
from its angle of neutral clarity.

Poem for Lake Michigan

That first week of elementary school
I stood at the corner

after the bell rang—wondering
which way to turn—

what direction was home?
Clueless among even grids

of flat, straight streets until
I realized it was the lake—inland sea

with high bluffs—the silver lapis or jade blue
ever-shifting distance of its surface

that told me: this way is *east*.
It was only ever the water

that gave me a hold on the earth,
told me which way to go.

Waiting Beside My Father

In the ICU room, ten days
where he coma-slept, arranged by the doctor
to rest his brain after the fall,
I sat beside him. I remember wearing
my slate-blue jacket with the big ruffle
at the collar, its cotton soft and somehow
reassuring on my body as I watched
the nurses glide by in the gleaming hallways,
and the kind hospitalist arrived with a lift
of hope in his voice. Inside me I felt a small, carved
chapel of patience I didn't know I possessed.
I closed my eyes, apologized to my father
for years of crabbiness between us.
I felt his brain smoothing out its frenzy, as if floating
on a long journey, as if a river
was carrying us, though
I had never learned to swim.

When My Mother Called

Always the same four words
to begin: *Hi, it's Mom honey*,
as if I could ever not recognize
tenderness when it arrived,
the well of kindness in a voice.
And the conversations
that might follow: What did you think
of that article? How is the new coat working out?
Oh you looked so beautiful!
I am loving your book.
I need to get groceries today.
I've been thinking of when you were young, and all
those years with your father, how sorry I am
I was so distracted by sadness then.
What time are you picking me up tomorrow?
I'll be waiting at the living room window;
no, that's okay, no need to get out of the car,
I'll be there, looking for you honey, always.

Returning to the Old Neighborhood After Thirty Years

Something beyond nostalgia led me back, thirty years
since now—so much sadness yet to be uncovered,
so much poetry yet to unfold. I'd walk the two blocks
from the elevated train to our russet brick building,
passing the elegant brownstones, their carved stonework
and courtyards deep in trees and shadow;
then the tall wrought-iron gate of the park
that collected the snow sifting down every winter,

before I'd dip into the secondhand bookstore
stacked everywhere with an unsorted feast.
It was there I first found Proust, packed into a three-volume
edition with tissue-thin crackling pages, where I first heard
the phrase lost time as if time could be found
and claimed, or even transformed
within the ache of the heart that holds it close.

Upon Waking

after Emily Dickinson

I'll tell you how the day began—

a dream-strand at a time—

the pictures sifted in gold-burgundy

the messages, like keys, were lost

For My Friend Gone On

with a phrase from Emily Dickinson

You left us quick,
you left us stunned,
and yet

under our nerves, sitting
Ceremonious as tombs,
comes a plot

of wonder—oh what
you must know now.

For the Thin Places

It seems I am forever
looking for the thin

place, wishing to glimpse
inside a moment, close enough

to stand sentry to the invisible.
I want to balance on a tight rope

between mystery and awe, be held
in the slim, glimmering pause

like the one just before
the singing is heard.

Eternity

Such an odd word
to use in the twenty-first century,

the woman said of my poems,
as if the word has gone

the way of manual typewriters,
poodle skirts, or rick-rack

on kitchen aprons like the ones
my beloved grandmother wore

back in the era,
the passing of her time

and more time, her life
gone the way of forever now.

The Notebooks of Other Women Poets

after Eavan Boland

I wonder if the silver spirals
of your notebooks become so worn
from the opening and shutting of your efforts
that pages begin slipping from their holds,

if you need the smoothest possible feel
of ivory pages against your palms,
a touch that might resemble a woman
pouring cream from a pitcher

in a portrait by some late Dutch painter,
where every shape is etched with gravity,
and light sifting through mullioned windows
seeks to burn through centuries.

Visiting the Brontës Again
After Twenty Years

Haworth, Yorköshire

Everything is waiting across
the sleep-dragged Atlantic–
moors and wild air, yellow gorse
and lichen, rain-stained stones,
the leaning graves guarding the entrance
to their home, and my persistent sense
of arrival at a long-dreamed upon meeting—
the sisters with patience as old as centuries,
as young as the first page of a story:
There was no possibility of taking a walk that day . . .

While in the Yorkshire Dales

After our meal of pulled pork and apple pie,
thick-cut chips and wilted greens, sated
to the marrow, we discovered still more—
outside, beside a swath of nodding daffodils—
a stepping stone bridge over gurgling waters.
We skipped, laughing, across to the other side,
a trail that wound through a moss haven of woods,
along a drystone fence to the highest hill
where we stopped. There, on top,
one massive sheep, poised like an empress,
detached and magnificent. Solitary, she
regarded us. We could hardly go
any further as we watched her
move not once from her wild throne.

Writerly Dream

George Murray Smith, of
Smith, Elder & Co., London, 1847

To have a book accepted
the way the bespectacled editor
leaned back in his creaking, leather chair
one Sunday morning; a manuscript unbound
from twine and brown paper on his lap.
He read and read until the lamps
outside his Cornhill office were lit;
scribbled a hasty note of apology
to the friend he could not meet after all, for he
could not stop reading. With only a sandwich
and a glass of wine for sustenance (*the meal,
a very hasty one*, he would later recall), the pages
and pages named *Jane Eyre* held him
long into the London night
and through the centuries to come.

The Last Unread Poems of Charlotte Brontë, March 2022

I am not a bird, and no net ensnares me. —Jane Eyre

To be unearthed at the International Antiquarian Book Fair—
no larger than a playing card, survived inside
some nineteenth-century schoolbook.

Who will vie for the priceless—
poor brown paper stitched with coarse thread, words
crossed out and corrected, infinitesimal
scratchings of a girl-woman announcing:

Attempts at rhyming of an inferior nature, Jane
not yet stirring, not yet tapping
from inside the egg
into an astounded world.

On the Burren

County Clare, Ireland

Peat smoke from somewhere,
horizontal rain, or else
a slow mist as you walk, and gray sky

lowering. Yellow-gold and purple
lichen holding fast to rock—
the great fields of limestone.

In the distance, you can hear
the tumbling of waves, you are on the edge
of the Atlantic after all.

An echoing vastness is everywhere—to love this place
you must be strong in yourself,
feel your soles grounded keenly to stone.

When Asked Why Do I Keep Wanting to Return to Ireland

I could begin with the silky pour
of the Guiness beside a peat fire in
a centuries-old pub with dark timbers;
I could say how the word *Connemara*
conjures my heart into a nest,
how wind and sky and breaking surf off the coast
of Mullaghmore make me lean toward wild joy
alongside bogs and stones, and the remembrance
of the last phone call with my mother before she died—
across the wild Atlantic, our crackling connection
from Kylemore Abbey where I stood by the shore
of the tiny lough—some days it is all
I know to remember, Ireland allowing me
to deepen and stand so near the gate
to the Otherworld, its misty latch shining.

After Learning My Friend Has Died

And so it begins,
the tallying backward
to remember: when was the last
telephone call, the last
text message, last email,
the last time seeing her face, her skin still
lovely smooth in her sixty-ninth year—
hearing her buoyant laughter that late
afternoon on her patio, September sun
lighting up the back of her head in the photo
she later joked finally made her
into some form of angelic being.

To This Day

for Rosemary

The calendar marks three weeks
to this day your heart
slowed to a crawl,
then stopped.
Three weeks that might be
three hundred years
or none at all—
there are no in betweens,
no middle grounds
in this land of your leaving.

After My Friend's Death, Her Husband Tells Me to Take Whatever I Want from Her Bookshelves

No matter that I already have more
than can fit on my own shelves,
I want her Irish poets, with translations,
the old novelists she raved about—Mary Stewart
and Nancy Mitford; her thick and weighty softcover
Remembrance of Things Past, and the writers to place me
in the center of poetry's spirit: *Rules for the Dance*,
Poemcrazy, and *Nine Gates*.
On the topmost shelf I found a corner of my own
slim volumes, lined up at attention the way she
always listened; inside, inscriptions I'd long forgotten
I'd scribbled, though repeating what I've always
known all along: *for my sister friend and rescuer, you also
helped make these words live.*

My Friend's Heart

I am thinking of it now, giving
one last effort while she slept,
in quiet, claiming enough.
In the morning her husband said
he found contentment on her face,
calm beauty, as if the sunrise
had found its home as she stepped through.

A List

for Rosemary

Today I tried making a list
of all the places we gathered
together: Lombardinos for Italian,
LaBrioche for biweekly poetry tea,
Bubble Up Bar for nightcaps,
the bookshops where you'd sit front row
whenever I gave a reading.

And I will never not see you
settling onto your living room side chair
while waiting for your signature Bolognese sauce
to find its final perfection for our dinners.
    There you are again—drawing your fingers upward
through your light hair as you make another
passionate point; your smile widening, ablaze—
you are looking at me as you speak, how easy it was
to love myself in that glow.

How She Might Have Left

Through the revolving door,

the turnstile,

past the swinging gate,

through the sluice gate,

across stepping stones over water,

over the threshold

into the next element

past air and water

and sight—she has stitched herself

with seams of light.

Christmas List for Santa

after Jack Ridl

Cathedral elms arching over the boulevards of my childhood

Face-to-face with John Keats's very *striking countenance*

An afternoon nap inside a mound of October leaves

A cup of coffee staying hot forever

Conversations without spatterings of *it's like*

Mornings always light at 5 a.m.

In my sleep, the sound of waterfalls

Emily Brontë's moon over my house

Crumbs from my yaya's cookies sticking to my fingertips

That second just after I pick up the wall phone to hear again
my mother's first hello

Holding my balance in a world, sorrow-seeped,
like a prima ballerina on one toe

Daughter, Leaving Again

The way of
our days now,
the way of
our years, the coming
and going,
joining and splitting,
arrivals and departures—
in my heart, loss
and accrual, like the gradual
luster of the nacre becoming.

For the Tiny Spider Squashed Inside the Pages of Poems by Mary Oliver

I wonder at your curiosity—what were you
searching for in your one tiny
and precious life, inside a used and musty
paperback edition of poetry?
Did it happen in winter when the silence
of deep snow granted peace to all creatures,
or was it a morning in mid-August when blackberries
hung like jewels in the brambles and woods
and the dark creeks were bursting,
    when summer was brimming over with its own
exuberance, spilling over so that you paused to linger
just a little longer, lost in a reverie of beauty,
staying just one page too long.

Praise Song for My Mother

after Grace Nichols

You were belonging—
    quilted and warm and threaded strong

You were the moonstone's gleam

The scent of lilac just before waking

You were talisman, marker—

    The song in the tree

    The ink in the pen that flows toward the poem

The Presence of One Word

I read *jacaranda* in a poem,
a tree abundant and ordinary
where my daughter lives across the country
from her childhood now;
her favorite tree she tells me,
and I see why, just saying *jacaranda*—
the way the silk blossoms
of its syllables sweep
and bound and flutter
then slightly fall
as if the trees
my daughter loves now
have introduced themselves
to me here, for this moment
of time away from her,
in a poem.

On Being Asked Again if My Daughter Is an Only Child

She is not the only,
she is the one,
containing multitudes.

Our hearts were crammed as full as yours.
There was no lack in our house,
though maybe fewer partitions
with pure light overflowing
through every expansive room.

Fiona Penelope in the World

Roused from her morning nap
and unzipped from her fleecy cocoon,
she joins us. Balanced
on her mother's lap,
the look on her face—
cherry-infused cheeks,
brown saucers of eyes—
her smile is something beyond happiness,
as if the egg of Wonder was cracked open
and spilling its secret astonishments.

Song of the Lark

    Jules Adolphe Breton,
    Art Institute of Chicago

Is it dawn or dusk?
Is she beginning or done with her day?
Her scythe is paused in midair as she listens,

feet bare to the dirt,
a partial disc of an orange sun behind her,
sky bleeding to coral and rose.

I cannot tell if she is worrying
or simply amazed.
The fields beyond are a green deepening.

I want to believe it is morning,
the first prayers of the hour in that song.

When the Consolation of a Word Comes to You

Not *detach*, which sounds too much
about the retina, and this is not about the eye

but the heart and its gates—
unlatch and allow yourself to roam

beyond what is hurting you, further into the fields
and meadows—there, find a spot

to kneel down in the deep, fragrant grasses,
make a bed for your body where the summer
is still singing your name.

At the Green Sanctuary and Natural Path Cemetery

for Rosemary

I'm lost on the narrow trails sloping
and curving among the exuberant green of late May.

I suppose my friend is everywhere here,
and that is the point: growing into the earth

now, indistinguishable from fern or maple,
oak or ash. Birdsong crisscrosses

everywhere as I make my way deeper
into the woods. It is supposed to be enough;

I might be too set or greedy, I want more—
one marker with dates chiseled

or raised in burnished bronze.
I want a stone that endures for her name.

Walking the Brontë Moor in Spring

Get your naggy self out there, start
along the public footpath, past the barns
and their newborn lambs curled up in the yards;

begin at the top, alongside tall, bent grasses and gorse,
browned heather and stones and crags—past
Penistone Hill and the reservoir. The wind

is wider up there, let yourself walk
for unmeasured time, the moor air
erase your every last edge.

Girls at the Piano

    Renoir, 1892

What draws my attention
is not what music the girls
might be playing,
but their long hair
pulled back from their rose-
tipped faces the way a bow
is tied at the back of a gown,
all the sumptuous fabric flowing
and falling, strands of sunburnt wheat
and russet leaves, the way autumn's heart
has found its rhythm in their hair.

To Do, Morning

after Brian Doyle

I will wake in the morning and listen for the cardinal.
I will slip on the warm socks I laid aside the evening before.
I will lift and billow the bed covers, tidy them into a smooth
    field for the dog to jump up on during the day.
I will hold the banister so as not to slip on the carpeted stairs
    as I descend to make my coffee.
I will lean near to the pot so I can breathe
    deeply the scent of the dark grounds.
I will listen for the first gurgle and drip that signals
    my morning's desire will soon be in hand.
I will just then notice a fragment of a dream
    floating past me in the kitchen air.
I will stand a moment in silence for all I have
    forgotten in the nights and also in the days,
    the dreams and presences living
      their wondrous, irrepressible lives without me.

Coffeehouses in Vienna

You may order cafe melange,
einspanner, grosser brauner,

a Maria Theresa served with orange liqueur
and whipped cream.

Under the vaulted ceilings
and polished old woods,

marble tables will hold your apfelstrudel
with vanilla custard, your sachertorte,

Dobos torte, or rum sponge.
Waiters in long tailcoats glide from place

to place, letting you stay as long
as you dream. Grandeur

seeps into your once stagnant thought;
you have placed yourself in the dignity

of the coffee hour—what goes on and on and on,
the deep cup of time in your palms.

In Mozart's Apartment

Vienna

No matter that the popular
guidebook author claims:
*Today, the actual apartment
is pretty boring*,
still you go, the rooms
mostly empty but for paintings
and displays on the walls,
yet the wide-planked wooden floorboards
are the same he walked on
for three years in the later
part of the 1700s; and the six-paned glass
with the same view he saw
down to the cobblestones
of Domgasse in Stephansplatz,
which is all you are thinking about
as you wander the seven rooms of
his best years with wife Constanz,
where the Haydn quartets were born,
piano concertos, *The Marriage of Figaro*,
and so much more—the air
you are breathing right now
surely still keeps some stray atoms
of his genius and his joy.

Reading the Spanish Poets

I like arriving at my neighborhood cafe
under a still-dark sky of an early
December morning, the air trembling
with a secret anticipation
as if a quiet gift
is about to be opened, the ribbon
already fallen to the floor.

January Sighting

Lone figure on the lake surface

inscribing the ice–twirling

and tumbling winter into a kind of song.

I watch her gliding further and further out

dissolving into a silver distance—

trusting what holds her to hold.

Another Mid-Range Hotel

The walls breathe beige,
wall-to-wall carpet mottles gray,
faux-paneling hides
a mini fridge somewhere.

Oh give me an ochre-red wall
with stencilings of hibiscus.
Give me a paisley rug,
a curved seashell lampshade
giving off amber-rose glow
that enables me to wonder

whether I have stepped into
a twentieth-century salon
or a fortune teller's nest
who will promise me a long
and vibrant life, beyond

purgatories of location
so terrified of offending,
so very far from anywhere.

In the Morning Quiet I Hear My Mother Speaking

She is telling me
to take the slim volume of poems
out from its place
between my red bookends;
a chapbook from years ago
I'd almost forgotten,
something about a mother's heart
in its title. She is telling me the words
will be there, to open it and press flat
the middle pages with my palm; she says there
will be a bench for her and me to rest upon.

My Mother and Gratitude

In those last years before the cancer took over—
her feet were always cold—she kept drawers full
of socks, the cozy fleecy kind I loved to find for her.
She'd scuffle a bit as she walked, saying to me, "Honey,
your mother's body is falling apart!" then she'd shrug or
    giggle
as she crossed from her living room to the tiny kitchen
where she might pour herself a soda, or brew a potful
of hazelnut roast for us to share when I'd sleep over,
her feet always thickly padded with two or even three
pairs of socks, pale pink and lavender, ivory with navy stripes,
it didn't matter what they looked like, she loved every pair
my sister and I gave her for birthdays, Christmas, Mother's
    Days,
and in between, any small thing, she would thank us and
    thank us
again, as if we'd made another day easier for her somehow,
as if we'd given her the world.

Finding My Grandmother on a Greek Island

Sifnos

I followed the aroma up the narrow
street of Apollonia, twin village to Artemonas,
up toward the whitewashed walls of a house,
one of so many with the blue shutters
and doors, blue like a being in itself.
Through the open door—an ivory cloth
with hand-done tatting trailed along
the edges of a dining room table,
a bowl of red eggs in the center (eggs
dyed for Christ's blood). I moved
a few steps; the kitchen's casement window
angled out where I stood near—held by the sound
of someone humming and chopping, perhaps onions,
beans, or leeks to include in Easter supper,
a kapama sauce simmering from someplace
in the past behind her, everything
set in motion for the family to arrive.

Morning Gladness

after Denise Levertov

The window raised just enough
for the first songs to float in,
    sway me between waking
and sleep
and first light—fluid gold
through sheer drapes.
Illumination is waking—
each thing given to my eye

Title Index

A Belated Thank You to Miss Joanne Martins of Cathedral Square Publishing Company in Milwaukee, Wisconsin, circa 1971 16
After Learning My Friend Has Died 41
After My Friend's Death, Her Husband Tells Me to Take Whatever I Want from Her Bookshelves 43
Against Despair 20
A List 45
Another Mid-Range Hotel 64
Assistance 14
At the Green Sanctuary and Natural Path Cemetery 56
Christmas List for Santa 47
Coffeehouses in Vienna 60
Daily Practice 13
Daughter, Leaving Again 48
Eternity 33
Finding My Grandmother on a Greek Island 67
Fiona Penelope in the World 53
For My Friend Gone On 31

For the Thin Places 32
For the Tiny Spider Squashed Inside the Pages of Poems by
   Mary Oliver 49
Girls at the Piano 58
Go Where the Door Is Open, She Said 23
How She Might Have Left 46
In Mozart's Apartment 61
In the Morning Quiet I Hear My Mother Speaking 65
January Sighting 63
Late Apology 25
Making the Greek Meatballs 19
Midwestern Summer 24
Morning Gladness 68
My Friend's Heart 44
My Mother and Gratitude 66
On Being Asked Again if My Daughter
   Is an Only Child 52
On Our Way to My Grandfather's Village 18
On the Burren 39
Poem for Lake Michigan 26
Praise Song for My Mother 50
Quiet in Winter 22
Reading the Spanish Poets 62
Returning to the Old Neighborhood After Thirty Years 29
Song of the Lark 54
The Last Unread Poems of Charlotte Brontë,
   March 2022 38
The Notebooks of Other Women Poets 34
The Presence of One Word 51
Threshold 21
To Do, Morning 59
To This Day 42
Upon Waking 30
Visiting the Brontës Again After Twenty Years 35
Waiting Beside My Father 27

Walking the Brontë Moor in Spring 57
When Asked Why Do I Keep Wanting
   to Return to Ireland 40
When My Mother Called 28
When the Consolation of a Word Comes to You 55
While in the Yorkshire Dales 36
Writerly Dream 37
Yaya's Dresser 17
Yaya's Telephone 15

First Line Index

A
  After our meal of pulled pork and apple pie 36
  Always the same four words 28
  And so it begins 41

C
  Cathedral elms arching over the boulevards
   of my childhood 47

E
  Everything is waiting across 35

G
  Get your naggy self out there, start 57

I
  I am thinking of it now, giving 44
  I could begin with the silky pour 40
  I followed the aroma up the narrow 67
  I like arriving at my neighborhood cafe 62
  I'll tell you how the day began 30

I'm lost on the narrow trails sloping 56
In the ICU room, ten days 27
In those last years before the cancer took over 66
I read *jacaranda* in a poem 51
Is it dawn or dusk? 54
It seemed to reign 17
It seems I am forever 32
I will wake in the morning and listen for the cardinal ...59
I wonder at your curiosity—what were you 49
I wonder if the silver spirals 34

L
Lone figure on the lake surface 63

M
My grandmother wept at her kitchen sink 20

N
No matter that I already have more 43
No matter that the popular 61
Not *detach*, which sounds too much 55

P
patting meat into small mounds 19
Peat smoke from somewhere 39

R
Roused from her morning nap 53

S
She is not the only 52
She is telling me 65
Some mornings all I do 13
Something beyond nostalgia led me back, thirty years 29
Such an odd word 33

T
That first week of elementary school 26
That January day I stood 21
The calendar marks three weeks 42

The quickest way to the pool 24
The walls breathe beige 64
The way of 48
The window raised just enough 68
This winter quiet 22
Through the revolving door 46
To be unearthed at the International Antiquarian
   Book Fair 38
Today I tried making a list 45
To have a book accepted 37
to the gleaming fat June bug 25
Turn away from 23

W

Weighty and black, substantial 15
We stalled in traffic—a line of goats 18
What draws my attention 58
When I pick up my pen 14

Y

You left us quick 31
You may order cafe melange 60
You must have guessed how, at eleven years old,
   I craved 16
You were belonging 50

www.ingramcontent.com/pod-product-compliance
Lightning Source LLC
Chambersburg PA
CBHW010047090426
42735CB00020B/3419